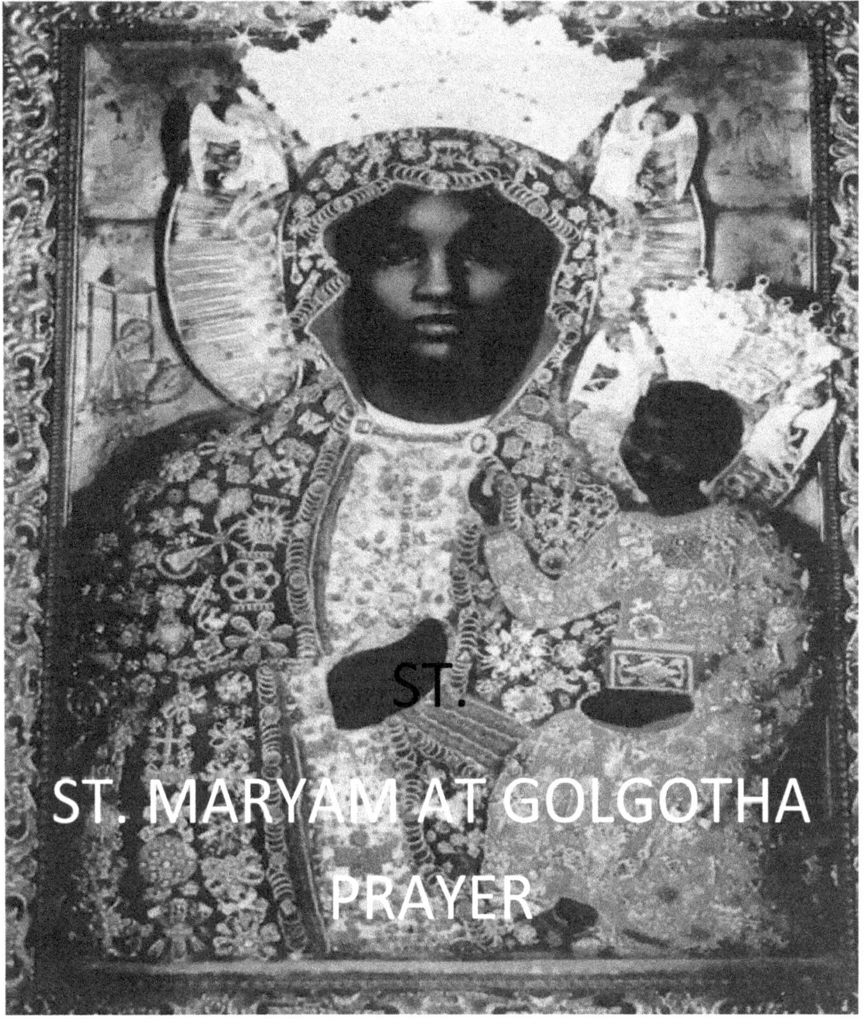
ST.
ST. MARYAM AT GOLGOTHA
PRAYER

Published by Lulu

ISBN: 978-0-244-48487-3

5/13/19

By Waheba Selassie

The Throne of David

This was Establish as the Imperial Coat of Arms of Ethiopia. Showing the Monarchy of Christ, this went to Ethiopia with St. Maryam of Zion of the Tribe of Judah!

The Holy Trinity

Qedus Selassie

Is now Revealed!

As Qedamawi Haile Selassie

Holding the Orb in His Hand

The Holy Trinity Crowned St. Maryam, And the Father, the First of the Holy Trinity Holding the Orb in His Hand

Yahshua Christ in One with the Father and the Holy Spirit Came to Earth And Was Crucify For Our Sin!

“Behold the Hand, Behold the Nail”

TO MY BELOVED GOD SON; GABRE MENFES QIDUS

SERVANT OF THE HOLY TRINITY

Formerly: Ras Seymour

TO WHOM I AM SO MUCH INDEBTED

IN THIS PRESENT WORK

AT THE 13, ON THE 13, OF THE 13, IN THE 13 AND FOR THE 13

AS HOLY MARY WITH 12 STARS ON HER HEAD

YAHSHUA CHRIST WITH 12 APOSTLES

HAILE SELASSIE NAME WITH 13 LETTERS

A DEVOTED ORTHODOX CHRISTIAN AND HEAD OF THE TEWAHEDO FAITH FORM AN EMBODIMENT OF THE FATHER AND THE SON AND THE HOLY SPIRIT THE HOLY TRINITY TRANSITION FROM RASTAFARI

OF A LIVING TABERNACLE OF THE HOLY TRINITY

A MYSTERY IS BEING REVEALED!

Foreword

These prayers are original from Ethiopia, Held in the Church in Glory and honor to the Pure Virgin, Holy Maryam the Mother of God and center of the Cross. But they were stolen and held in the British Museum, which then discovery by the Blessed Son of Our Lady; Gabre Menfes Qidus, formally, Ras Mclean. Unfortunely..., He was taken to prison and serve time; and after release fond with a rear disease call cancer. The big question is how did such poison get into his bone and body which was never there before?

Thanks be to Yahweh of Host, The Holy Trinity; Kidus Selassie, He will make it to the heavens in the general assembly of the Holy angels and saints in Mount Zion and his work will be rewarded as a great servant of the Most High God.

As it is clear that the force of evil in high and low places will continue to fight against the truth and held the people in bondage...,

Behold these prayers are now presented to the world, as every human being should know the truth of the Holy Virgin MARYAM and the important part She play in our life to Salvation. None should be left out of a copy of these prayers because of the information contained within.

I pray that all would come to the revelation of the Holy Virgin MARYAM Mother of God to the embodiment of the Holy Trinity of WeAb Wewold Wemenfes Qidus Ahahdu Amlak; these words in fact are Ethiopian and means:

(The Father, The Son and The Holy Spirit One God)

Many symbolisms are in the Holy Bible which relates to the Holy Virgin MARYAM, before She was born. St. Maryam is one of the hidden mysteries of Yahweh of Host. And Her body did not see corruption as CHRIST took on Flesh from Her being the Center of the Cross and Mother of all Christian. He did not see corruption. So the Root and the Offspring live on. And when we are Baptize in the Holy Name of the Trinity we become One again in this union. And Adam who was slain from the foundation of the world, is Re-born in Christ because of the Pure Virgin MARYAM. Blessed be Her Holy Name from generation to generation and world without end. Amen!

PREFACE

THE PRAYER WHICH THE HOLY VIRGIN ST. MARYAM MADE ON THE MOUNTAIN OF GOLGOTHA, WHICH IS THE TOMB OF YAHSHUA ON THE 21ST DAY OF THE MONTH SANE JUNE 26TH

TABLE OF CONTENTS

CHAPTER 1

THE PRAYER WHICH THE VIRGIN MADE ON THE MOUNTIAN OF GOLGATHA, WHICH IS THE TOMB OF YAHSHUA ON THE 21ST DAY OF THE MONTH SANE (JUNE 26TH)

THIS PRAYER IS VERY IMPORTANT TO ALL ORTHODOX CHRISTIAN, AS WELL AS TO OTHERS SEEKING THE TRUTH OF THE HOLY TRINITY!

[FOR THE ETHIOPIAN TEXT SEE BRIT, MUS. MS, HARTL. 5471 AND FOL. 39 F, AND ADD. NO. 16, 233 (DILLMANN, CATALOGUS, NOS. L111 AND L1X AND BRIT, MUS. MS ORIENT, NO. 639 (WRIGHT, CATALOGUE, NO. LXXXV, P. 52), FOR A FRENCH TRANSLATION, SEE BASSET, OP. CIT., P. 11F.]

"My LORD and my God, my Son and my king, Yahsua the Christ, who of thine own free will was born of me, who didst suck milk from my breasts, whom the heavens cannot contain, whom the bounds of the world cannot contain, whom the earth cannot carry, whose hand the space of the abyss, and the depths of the sea, and the rain-floods cannot fill, whom the angels and the powers of heaven cannot draw night, my son and my king, I Maryam thy Mother, thy servant, beseech and make supplication to thee. I carried thee In my womb for nine months and five days. Thou hast dwelt in my body, thou have sucked milk from my breasts and hath lives upon my milk for three years, and I carried thee on my back for five years. Remember, O LORD, that I have gone about with thee for thirty years, and that I fled with thee from one country to another when Herod wanted to slay thee. Hear my prayer, O my LORD, and my petition, O my LORD, my God. Remember, LORD, that I carried thee in my womb for nine months and five days, and remember that thou hast sojourned in my body. Remember, LORD that I gave birth to thee in Bethlehem during the season of ice and snow, remember, LORD that I left my country and went about with thee from one country to another. Remember, LORD, my exile in a foreign land, and how I suffered hanger, and thirst, and wretchedness. Is there no reason for interesting thee on behalf of the sinners as well as for the righteous who have celebrated my commemoration? my LORD, hearken to the prayer and petition which i set before me that thou wouldst hear my words of entreaty and fulfill all that is in my heart this day [I beseech thee] to send unto me forthwith twelve angels of mercy who shall tarry with me, and fulfill all that is in my heart, and the petitions for acts of grace which my lips make to thee.

I beseech thee, O my Son and beloved one by God, thy Father, who was with thee before the creation of the world.

I beseech thee by Christ, thy name which was with thee, before the creation of the heavens and the earth and of the angels and men, and of the sun, moon and stars, and before the night was separated from the day.

I beseech thee by the Paraclete, the Holy Spirit, who hath come forth from thy father, and who proceedeth from thee, and who was with the father and the son before the stars of the evening, and the stars of the morning made their appearance.

I beseech thee by [my] womb wherein I carried thee for nine months and five days.

I beseech thee by [my] bosom, O my Son, whereon thou didst lie.

I beseech thee, O my beloved Son, by [my] breasts which thou dids suck for three years.

I beseech thee by [my] back which hath carried thee for five years.

I beseech thee, O my beloved Son, by the hunger and thirst which I suffered for thy sake when we fled from Herod and went into the land of Egypt.

I beseech thee by the tears which gushed from my eyes and fell on thy glorious flesh.

I beseech thee by the mouth which kissed thee.

I beseech the tongue which speaks with thee.

I beseech thee by my ears which heard thy gracious words.

I beseech thee by my feet which walked with thee for four and twenty years.

I beseech thee by the bed on which thou didst sleep.

I beseech thee by the clothes wherein thou were wrapped, O fire of the Deity.

I beseech thee by MICHAEL, the angel of thy wisdom.

I beseech thee by GABRIEL, the envoy of thy birth, who announced to me the glad tiding that I was to bear thee.

I beseech thee, by RAFHAEL, the angel of mercy.

I beseech thee, by URIEL, the angel of protection and salvation.

I beseech Thee by SALAKIYAL, the comforter of the sorrowful

I beseech thee, by SADAKIYAL the righteous and just

I beseech thee, by ANANYAL, the angel of mercy.

I beseech thee, by the four beasts, each having six wings and many eyes, which bear thy throne.

I beseech thee, by the Ninety-Nine Order of angels who serve thee

I beseech thee, by the ten thousand angels on thy right hand.

I beseech thee, by the ten thousand angels on thy left hand.

I beseech thee, by the ten thousand of angels who stand before thee.

I beseech thee, by the ten thousand of angels who stand behind thee.

I beseech thee, by the tens of thousands of tens of thousands of angels who surround thee.

I beseech thee by the vast spaciousness of the havens.

I beseech thee by the great extent of the earth.

I beseech thee by the angels of the clouds.

I beseech thee by the angels of the sun.

I beseech thee by the angels of the hills and mountains, who were in being before their abodes were created.

I beseech thee by the angels of fire.

I beseech thee by the heavens, which are thy throne.

I beseech thee by the earth, thy footstool.

I beseech thee by Jerusalem, thy city.

I beseech thee by mount tabor whereon were transfigured thy form and similitude.

I beseech thee by Mount Zion.

I beseech thee by the mount of Oliver, the door of thy kingdom.

I beseech thee by john, who baptizes thee.

I beseech thee by the Holy Spirit.

I beseech thee by the Holy Cross.

I beseech thee by the nails driven through thy hands and feet.

I beseech thee by thy holy body and glorious blood.

I beseech thee by thy passion and death.

I beseech thee by the dwelling in the dowels of the earth for three days and three nights.

I beseech thee by thy entrance among the dead.

I beseech thee by thy descent into Sheol.

I beseech thee by thy resurrection from the dead on the Third Day.

I beseech thee by thy ascension into heaven with great glory.

I beseech thee by thy second coming.

I beseech thee by the exaltedness of thy abode.

I beseech thee by thy years which never end.

I beseech thee by Iyuel, thy name which overcome the enemy.

I beseech thee by thy Name Seka.

I beseech thee by Egziabeher, thy name before the creation of the world.

I beseech thee by thy hidden name, which cannot be uttered.

I beseech thee by thy revealed name, which is unknown (?).

I beseech thee by SADOR.

I beseech thee by 'ALADOR.

I beseech thee by 'ADERA.

I beseech thee by DANAT.

I beseech thee by RODAS.

I beseech thee by SIDA'El.

I beseech thee, O my beloved Son, to dwell with me, that the gates of the prisons may open of themselves, that the power of the devils may be removed from every place wherein they are, that the powers of darkness may be expelled, that the abodes of idols may become like water [courses], that all the temples of false god may be laid waste, that their images may be broken in pieces, that all idols may be smashed, and that all the power of darkness may be destroyed. And I would that all the bonds of sins may be undone. And let all those who have had faith in this prayer be delivered from sin and see free by the voice, and by the voice of the Paraclete, the Holy Spirit, whose month (sic) is sharper that the razor (knife ?), which separateth on root from another, and the soul from the body. O my beloved Son, I beseech and entreat thee to hearken unto the words of my prayer, and to come with me, and fulfill everything which is in my heart.

when our Lady, the Virgin Maryam, had thou spoken, the earth quaked, the rock split asunder, the tombs revealed themselves, and the doors that were shut opened of themselves; and the twelve ranks of angels, following their captains, came down from heaven. And with them there came our LORD and Saviour Eyesus Kristos, who had with him ten thousand times ten thousand angels, ten thousand on his right hand, ten thousand on his left hand, ten thousand before him, and ten thousand behind him. There were seven light before him and seven light behind him, and fourteen lights which were brighter than ten thousand suns and moons, before his face.

at the sight of these our Lady Mary was seized with great fear, and she fell down upon the ground as one dead, then our LORD and Saviour Eyesus Kristos stretched out his hand, and raising her up made her to stand before him. And he said, "My Mother, what hath happened? Why weepest thou? – Thou who didst carry me in thy womb and on thy back. What hath frightened thee and terrified thee so greatly that thou hast fallen to the ground?" The blessed Mary answered and said to her beloved Son, "I have never before seen thee thus; I who have carried thee in a mortal body now see thee [enveloped] in a mighty power of fire. Formerly when I saw thee, thou hast the form of a man, but now I see thee having a terrifying and mighty appearance." Our LORD answered and said unto her, "O my mother, who didst carry me in thy womb for nine months and five days, who didst carry me on thy back and did feed me with the milk of thy breasts, sweeter than honey and sugar, whiter than the milk [of other women], flowing more freely that the water of the garden of Eden, what can I do for thee? For what work hast thou called me, O Maryam, and my mother? What petition can I grant? What can I do for thee?"

"And the blessed Virgin said unto her beloved Son, my LORD Eyesus Kristos, my God, my Saviour, and my king! Thou are my hope, my asylum, and my strength; in thee do I put my trust. I was strengthened by thee when I was in the womb of my Mother, and thou didst protect me therein, and of thee will I make mention at all times and forever. And thou were born of me by thy own free will, and with the permission of thy father and the Holy Spirit now, O LORD, hearken thou unto my prayer and petition, and incline thine ears to the words which my mouth shall utter. I am thy mother and thy servant, I beseech thee to build indestructible habitations of light for those who shall celebrate commemorations of me, and shall build churches in my Name. do thou array in the apparel of the heavenly marriage feast, and dress in the panoply of justice, which shall not wear out, which is fair to look upon and hath not been made by human hands, the man who shall clothe a naked man in my Name. Visit with thy mercy and compassion the man who shall visit the poor in my Name. Set, thou at thy heavenly table, O LORD, the man who shall feed him that is hungry and give drink to the thirsty in my Name. Make thou to drink of the river of the water of life which floweth in the Garden of Eden the man who shall nourish him that is famished in my Name. Comfort thou him that comforteth the suffering one in my Name, and comfort him when his soul shall depart from his body. LORD, make to rejoice the man who cheereth him that is sad, and set him among all the saints who please thee and fulfill thy will. Write thou in the book of life with a pen of gold, the Name of him that writeth this book, or who hath a copy thereof made. Bestow thou, O LORD, upon the man who suspendeth this prayer from his neck a reward, the like of which the eye of man hath never seen, nor the ear of man hath never heard of, nor the heart of man hath ever imagined.

I beseech ant entreat thee, LORD to deliver from hell everyone who believeth on me. Make him that shall sing my praises on the day of my festival, to hear the songs of the celestial chores of angels."

And the LORD said unto Her, "It shall be even as thou sayest. I will build habitations of light, and give a glorious seat in the kingdom of the heavens, and obtain the grace of my father and the Holy Spirit for him that shall build a church dedicated to thee.

The man who shall visit the sick in thy name I will visit when he is sick and prostrate on his bed. When he departeth from this fleeting world I will not make him to drink of the bitterness of the cup of death, and I will never forsake him until he hath arrived in the kingdom of heaven. If evil spirits essay to seize him, I will be his defender on the day of his tribulation.

The man who hath clothed the naked in thy Name, I will array in the inviable apparel of life, which will neither fray nor wear out, and I will crown him with an eternal and everlasting crown.

The man who hath given bread to the starving in thy Name I will feed on the bread which is not makes with human hands.

The man who hath given drink to the thirsty in thy Name I will make to drink a cup of the water of life which bubbleth up in the Garden of Eden, and which is sweeter than honey and sugar.

The man who hath comforted the afflicted in thy Name will I comfort when he Is a sufferer from grief and pain. The man who hath made the sad to be cheerful through thee I will make to rejoice in my kingdom and in that of my heavenly father.

I will write in the book of life the name of the names of him or her that shall have caused to be written, or shall themselves write the praises of thee.

I will light in the kingdom of heaven for the man who hath given a lamp [to a church dedicated to thee]a lamp which shall shine seven times brighter than the sum in the kingdom of heaven[and be], like unto the moon [Isaiah xxx.26]

I will grant my favour before beings celestial and beings terrestrial to the man who shall give thy name to his daughter.

the place wherein this prayer is, or where they name is invoked, or where a commemoration of thee is celebrated, shall not be approached by the powers of evil spirits; and all the filthy hosts of darkness and the spirits that work evil shall flee far therefrom.

The might of the enemy shall neither attack nor prevail over the man who carrieth this prayer. the evil spirits shall not come nigh to him, and no foul or filthy spirit, and no spirit of the night of day, whether they make themselves visible by a thrust of a thorn , or by the stamp of the feet; or by a dream by night or by day; or by impurity(?) of bread, or by the foulness (?) of water or wine; or by drunkenness or wrath, whether it body sickness of headache, or toothache, or by a foul mouth or pain of the heart; of by small-pox or by disease in the hands and feet; or by deadly fever or by a running cold; or by stomach ache or by shivering; on sea or land, or among trees or rocks, or fire or water, by arrogance or pleasure, or merry-making or hatred; by the howlings of wild beasts or the cries of the birds, by the heat of the sun or the chill of ice and snow; by the blasts of wind, by the bites of dogs and snakes and cobras and scorpions; by the blazing of the fire and the flowing of blood; whether it be in the darkness of the night or in the light of day, none of these spirits shall attack the man who carrieth this prayer, and the evil eye shall pass him by. If a man recieteth this prayer thieves of grain shall not come nigh unto his fields to steal wheat or barley or any other crop. Even so shall it be in the case of the wild animals which attack by day or by night, and if they come upon him they shall not be able to harm him. And even so shall it be in the case of hail storms and the attacks of grasshoppers [locusts and such-like], for none of the above – mentioned evils can draw nigh to the man who carrieth this prayer. All those who carry this prayer shall be protected from murrain in his cattle, and drought, and disastrous capture [of beasts?]. And I will save him that carrieth this prayer from every calamity, and every kind of suffering, and he shall escape fatal Illness. If he be attacked by a disease that can be cured I will heal him quickly, and if he hath committed sins they shall be forgiven him. If his disease be incurable I will send to him angels of light who shall carry his soul to a place of light and bring it to me; the bad angels shall not go near him, and the spirits of evil that dwell in the third heaven shall not lay claim to him. I will lay claim to him and be his guide on the day of his trouble, and I will with him to my father and the Paraclete. And with me shall come the twelve ranks of angels wearing collars of gold, and bearing censers, and wearing rings of gold and rich apparel, and crowns of gold and spikenard in the form of the rainbow, some made of fire and some of lightning, into the fifth heaven, to receive the man who carrieth this prayer. I will take him upon my breast, and i will make him to traverse [in safety] the sea of fire and I will bring him before my throne. When the hosts of heaven see him they shall utter cries of joy, and they will wave their wings and strike the ground with their feet, and rejoice over him that hath carried this prayer.

O, my Mother, didst thou not comprehend what I speak in my gospel, saying, if a man who hath one hundred sheep loseth one of them, will he not leave the ninety-and-nine in the desert and go and seek the sheep which is lost? And when he findeth the sheep, he taketh it upon his shoulders, and rejoiceth over it more than over the ninety-and –nine which he hath not lost. Then he calleth his friends and neighbours and saith unto them, rejoice with me, for I have found the sheep which was lost. Verily I say unto you, there shall be more joy in heaven over one sinner who repenteth than over ninety-and nine righteous men who do not need repentance (Luke xv. 4-7). All the celestial hosts shall rejoice over him that hath carried this prayer. When his soul shall go forth from his body and he shall depart from this fleeting world, I will bring him to my holy mountain (Isaiah lvi.7), and I will make him to be acceptable to my father. Mercy, compassion, grace and everlasting gladness shall be where this prayer is. The places where this prayer is recited shall be free from the plague, and pestilence, and deadly diseases of every kind, no matter what their names may be. I will bless him that carrieth this prayer, and his wife, and his children, and all his possessions, [and I will grant him] everything which he shall ask in thy name by this prayer and by this writing whether washeth, or invoketh aid [against evil spirits] or drinketh, or lowereth his voice, or sprinkleth water in his house with a pure heart, and a right faith, doubting nothing. I will consider his prayer forthwith, and I will grant him his heart's desire. Michael and Gabriel shall go to him and minster unto him where so ever he may be; and all the hoists of angels shall come and watch over carefully him that shall carry this prayer. O my Mother, thou virgin Maryam, who didst give me birth, I thy partner hereby give thee everything, and bestow upon thee glory both in the heavens and upon the earth."

and the blessed virgin asked him, saying, "Dost thou say this, O my Son?" and the LORD Eyesus Kristos replied, "I swear unto thee, and I will not lie unto thee, O Maryam my Mother, I swear unto thee by YHWH, my Father, by Kristos, which is my Name; by the Paraclete, the Holy Spirit; by Michael, the angel of my wisdom; by Gabriel, who announce my birth; by the four Cherubims with six wings and many eyes who carry my throne; by the four-and-twenty sages, who cense my throne and praise the glory of my being; by the ten thousand angels who stand at my right hand; by the ten thousand who are before me; by the ten thousand who are behind me; and by the ten thousand who watch; by the first Adam, my first-born; by Abel and Seth, and Canan and Mahalaleel, and Enoch; by Yared, and methuselah, and Noah, with whom I made a covenant in the heavens and on the earth saying, 'I will never again destroy the earth by the waters of a flood' (gen. ix.11, 15) I swear unto thee by Melchisedek my priest and my type; by Abraham, my beloved; by Isaac, my servant; by Jacob, my holy one, in whom I planted 12 branches; by Judah; by Pharez, by Benjamin, by Levi, by Issachar; by the people of the twelve tribes of Israel; by all the holy and righteous fathers; and by Enoch and Elijah - [Moses], the writers of my commandments. I swear unto thee by the pure bowels wherein i dwelt for nine months and five days; by thy breasts whereat i drank milk which was sweeter than honey and sugar, and whiter than the water of Eden. I swear unto thee by the one hundred and forty thousand children of Bethlehem which Herod had slain for my sake; and by the fifteen prophets who have proclaimed my kingdom; and by my envoys the twelve apostles; and by my disciples who sacrificed their lives for my sake; by the heavens, my dwelling-place, and by the earth whereon my feet rest; by the nine-and ninety ranks of angels; by the flame of fire of my veil; by the heights of heaven which are my habitation; by the shedding of my blood and by the sorrow of my death; by my sojourn for three days in the womb of the earth; by my descent into heal by my going forth from the tomb; by my resurrection from the dead on the third day; by my ascension into heaven; by my second coming in great glory; by my holy body; by my holy blood; by Jerusalem [the city] set free; by Zion decorated with glory; by the Sabbath of the Christians whereon I was born, and baptized, and revealed my resurrection for life and salvation; by the holy church, the bride adorned; by mount Zion; by the mount of olives, the door of my kingdom; by Golgotha, my tomb; by mount tabor, my abode, whereon my transfiguration took place; by the Christian church, my bride; and by thy white and shining form. By all these things I swear unto thee, O virgin Maryam, my Mother, she didst being me into the world, that I will not deceive thee by my promise, that my work to thee shall not prove a lie, and that i will never forget the declarations which I have made unto thee. If a shrIne be built and dedicated to thy Name. I will dwell therein and will accept the sweet savour of its offerings as I accepted those of Abel, the righteous man."

The blessed Virgin answered and said unto him" blessed be thou as are thy Father and the Holy Spirit, O thou who has grated unto me all these things of thine own free will. Praise be unto thee, O LORD, and glory be to thy Kingdome, and to the life giving spirit. Praise be unto thee, Heavenly Father, now and always and for ever and ever. Amen."

Our LORD, having finished his converse with his mother, gave her the salutation of peace, and went up into heaven with great glory. And the virgin went back to her house with great joy, and she praised god, saying, "Blessed be thou, O LORD. May thy Holy Name be loosed and glorified, with thy Holy Father and Holy Spirit, for ever and ever. Amen."

ST. MARYAM OF ZION

IS ALSO A SYMBOL OF THE FEMALE SIDE OF YHWH!

BARING THE CHILDREN OF YHWH OF HOST OF ALL NATION, TRIBES, TONGUE AND PEOPLE IN HER ARMS

AND AS MOTHER AFRICA – ETHIOPIA

GIVEN BIRTH TO HUMANITY

FROM GENESIS TO REVELATION

MAY OUR HOLY MOTHER ST. MARYAM OF ZION

FOREVER BE BLESS FROM THIS TIME FORTH

AND FOREVERMORE!

AMEN! AMEN! AMEN!

BY WAHEBA SELASSIE

www.ingramcontent.com/pod-product-compliance
Ingram Content Group UK Ltd.
Pitfield, Milton Keynes, MK11 3LW, UK
UKHW020424310726
14060UKWH00021B/21

9 780244 484873